ANIMALS THAT HUNT IN THE DARK

NOCTURNAL ANIMAL BOOK 1ST GRADE

Children's Animal Books

Speedy Publishing LLC

40 E. Main St. #1156

Newark, DE 19711

www.speedypublishing.com

Copyright © 2017

All Rights reserved. No part of this book may be reproduced or used in any way or form or by any means whether electronic or mechanical, this means that you cannot record or photocopy any material ideas or tips that are provided in this book.

n this book, we're going to talk about the different types of animals that hunt in the dark. So, let's get right to it!

A leopard on the hunt at night.

WHAT IS A NOCTURNAL ANIMAL?

When the sun goes down, many types of animals head straight for the safety of their underground dens or burrows. However, there are some creatures that sleep all or most of the day and come out to hunt at nighttime. If an animal sleeps during the day and hunts at night, then that animal is called nocturnal.

Nocturnal Lemur of Madagascar.

Lots of animals that are nocturnal are mammals. Mammals are warm-blooded and frequently have fur. These two physical traits help them to stay warm when temperatures drop at night.

*Spectral Tarsier (Tarsius spectrum),
rare nocturnal animals.*

One of the reasons that some animals have adapted for hunting at night is because they don't have to fight for food with animals that hunt during daylight. For example, most types of birds hunt during the day. Birds and bats eat some of the same types of insects and fruits, so bats adapted to hunt at night so they wouldn't have to compete with so many birds for food.

Giant Indian Fruit Bat.

There are some types of birds that are nocturnal too. Your parents may have called you a *"night owl"* if you like to stay up late to watch television. Some species of owls are nocturnal, but human beings aren't. When it gets dark out, most human beings like to go to sleep. Nocturnal animals have an internal sense that wakes them up when the sun goes down. Because they hunt at night, they can sneak up on their prey. The cover of darkness helps them hide from animals that might want to eat them.

Common Barn Owl (Tyto Albahead)

Sometimes it's the environment that makes animals adapt to being awake at night. In the desert, the temperatures are too hot for animals to be comfortable during daylight hours. These animals sleep in their cooler dens during the day. When the sun goes down and it gets cooler out, it's time for their "day" to get started at night.

Fennec fox

CHARACTERISTICS OF NOCTURNAL ANIMALS

Nocturnal animals have special characteristics that help them survive in the dark. For example, it would be hard for a predator to see the owl butterfly at night due to its dark coloring. During the day, the owl butterfly sleeps and at night it comes out to hunt for its food.

Giant Owl Butterfly (Caligo Memnon).

It has two spots on its wings that look like the eyes of another nocturnal creature, the owl. Animals that might want to eat it, think they are seeing an owl so they back away.

Sometimes you can tell that an animal might be nocturnal because it has very large eyes so that it can see even when there's not much light. Lots of nocturnal animals also have very sensitive ears that can hear small noises in the dark. Some have a powerful sense of smell that helps them too. They can smell scents that are far away.

HUNTING BY NIGHT

Animals must hunt for food, but while they are hunting, other animals might catch them and eat them. Nocturnal animals use the darkness to hide from their enemies as they hunt for their own food.

Badger emerging at dusk.

Owl species that are nocturnal have very sharp night vision even in the lowest level of light. Some can hunt by just hearing sounds. Their velvety wings are so quiet that they can swoop down to grab their prey in their talons before the prey hears them flying down.

Barn owl in flight before attack.

Large cats such as leopards and other meat-eaters use their keen vision, sensitive hearing, and powerful sense of smell to track down their prey. Still others have special senses. For example, bats use sound in the form of echolocation to find their food. Some nocturnal snakes can sense another creature's body warmth and this is how they find their prey

Certain animals have special abilities that help keep them safe. An aardvark can dig into the ground faster than any other type of creature. Native to Africa, it's a nocturnal

mammal that hunts for termites to eat at night. If it hears a predator coming after it, it quickly digs a hole and goes underground to hide.

NIGHT VISION

For many nocturnal predators, their eyesight is their most important sense. They usually have large eyes that point forward on their faces. For example, pet cats and many types of large, wild cats are nocturnal.

Ocelot (*Leopardus Pardalis*)

When the level of light goes down, your pupils, which are the black parts of your eyes, get larger to let in more light. If you look carefully at your pet cat's eyes at night, you will notice that its pupils get very large. Cats' pupils expand to three times the area that the pupils in human eyes can. As a result, your pet cat can see up to six times better than you can in dim light.

Cats as well as crocodiles and sharks are all nocturnal animals that hunt at night. They also all have a special layer of cells in the structure of their eyes known as a tapetum lucidum. This layer is like a mirror that reflects light back into their

eyes so they can see extremely well even in very dim light. That's also what makes cats' eyes glow green or red if you flash a flashlight in their direction at night.

Crocodile eye as it appears in dark waters.

Fireflies

GLOWING IN THE DARK

Some nocturnal animals can create their own glow. Fireflies, which are a special type of flying beetle, are nocturnal. Chemical reactions cause their abdomens to glow. Fireflies use their glow to tell predators that they contain chemicals that don't taste good. They also use their glow to attract mates.

USING ECHOLOCATION

Some species of bats don't see well. They use echolocation to find their prey as they hunt at night. They make a stream of noises that sound like clicks as they fly through the air.

Long-eared bat or common long-eared bat (Plecotus auritus) using scheme echolocation.

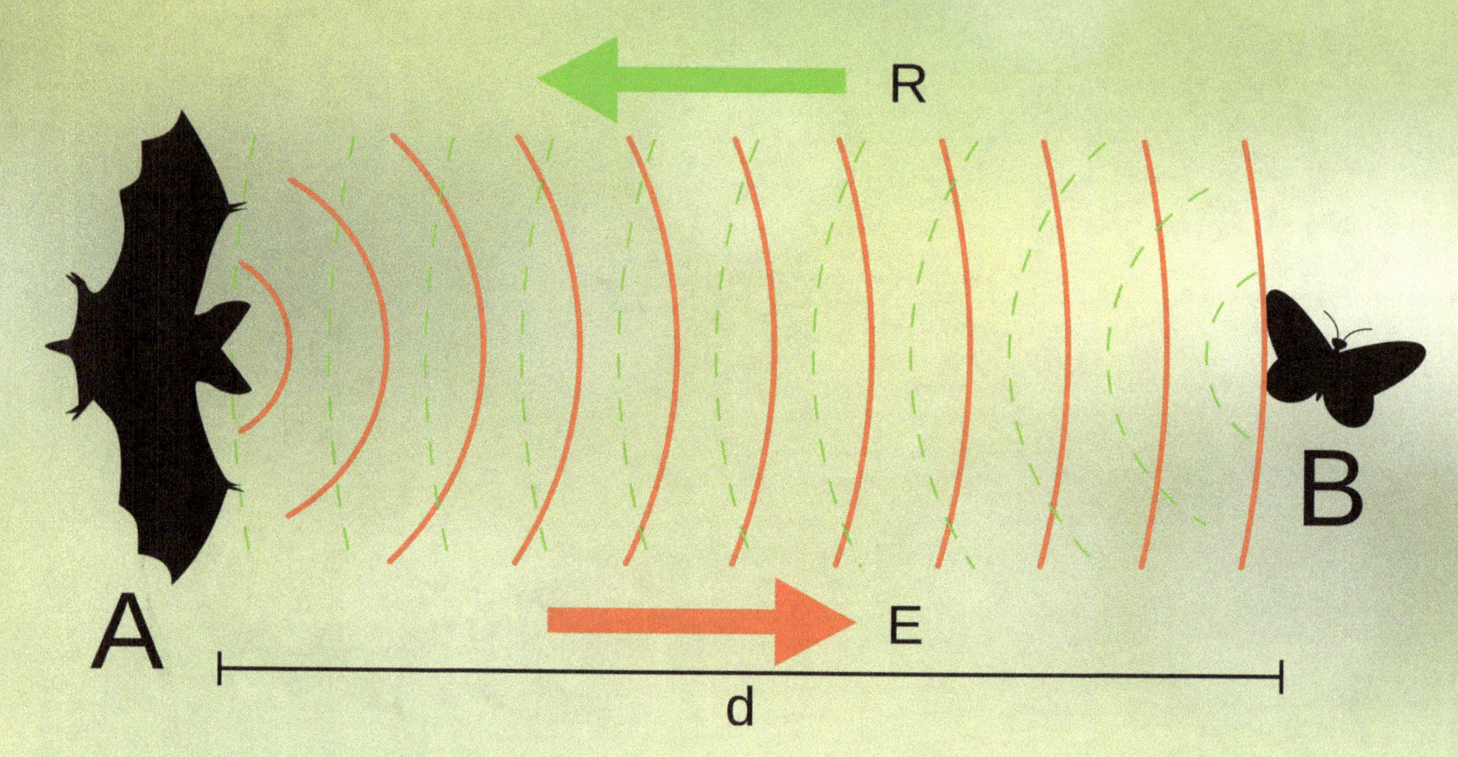

Chiroptera Echolocation.

These sounds bounce off objects such as flying moths and produce an echo that the bat can hear with its very sensitive ears. By listening to these returning echoes, the bat can figure out the location of its prey.

SOME ANIMALS THAT ARE NOCTURNAL

There are many different animals that are nocturnal. Here are a few you may recognize.

BAT

There are other mammals that can glide, but bats are the only mammals that can fly continuously. Some species are omnivores that eat insects. Others are herbivores, which means they eat plants, and some eat blood! There are

over 1000 different species of bats. Some bats prefer to live alone, and others live in caves as a community with thousands of other bats.

OPOSSUM

The Virginia or common opossum is a marsupial, which means it carries its offspring in a pouch. Its offspring are as tiny as bees when they're born. They crawl into their mother's pouch to be nourished and grow. As soon as they get large enough, they'll go in and out of her pouch.

Female Possum

As she hunts for food at night, they'll ride on her back. If a predator threatens an opossum, it will sometimes play dead by lying on the ground with its eyes tightly closed and its tongue sticking out.

Baby Opossum

OWL

Most birds are active during the day. Owls and nighthawks are exceptions. There are over 200 species of owls and many of them are nocturnal. Their forward-facing eyes give them binocular vision but they need to turn their heads to see in another direction.

Long-eared Owl

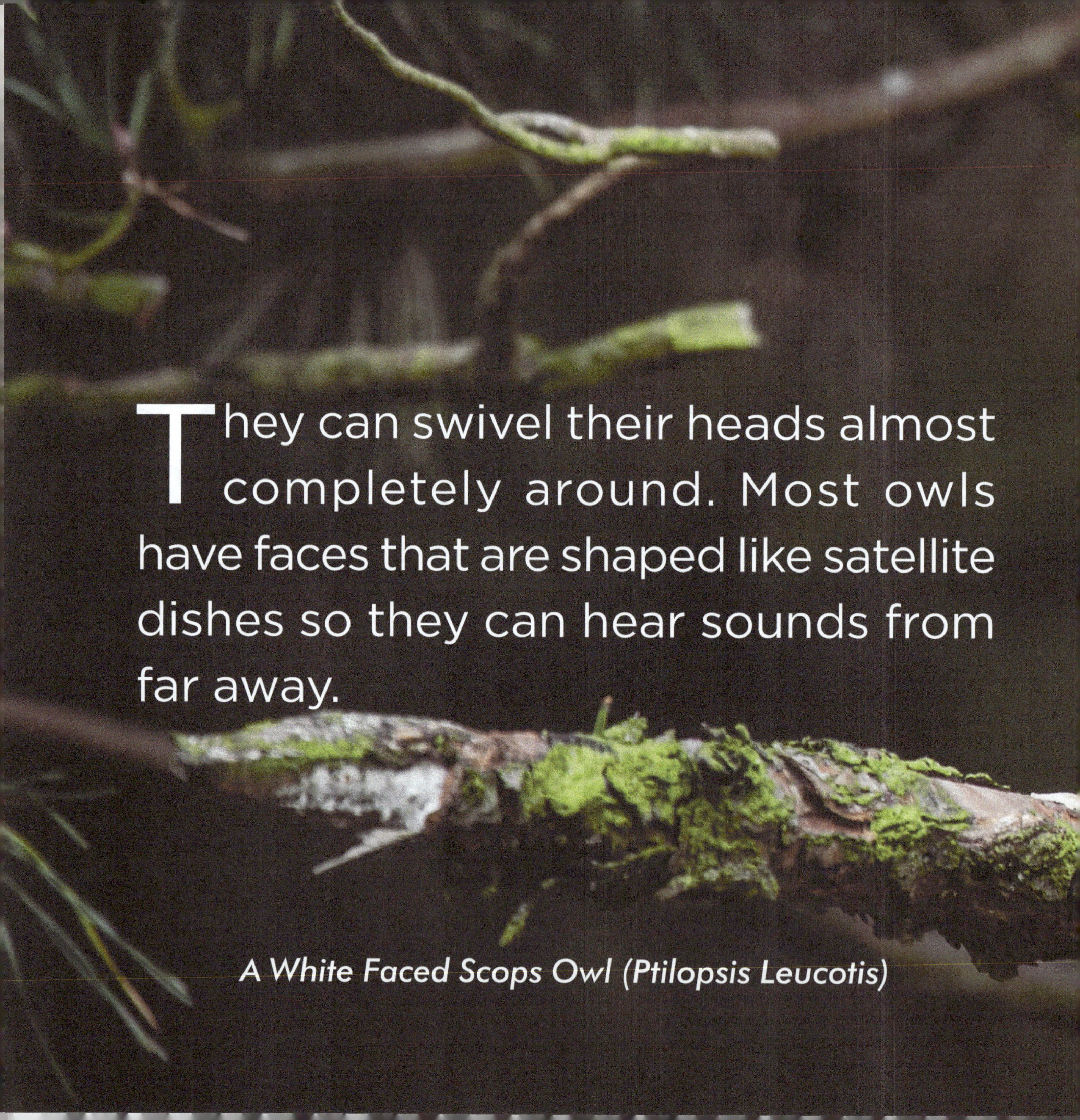

They can swivel their heads almost completely around. Most owls have faces that are shaped like satellite dishes so they can hear sounds from far away.

A White Faced Scops Owl (Ptilopsis Leucotis)

Raccoon

RACCOON

Raccoons are mammals that live in lots of different types of habitats. These adaptable animals live in forests, prairies, and marshes, but they've also adapted to human life and live in cities. It's a myth that raccoons wash their food.

When they catch food in the water, they do roll it over and over between their two highly sensitive hands. Raccoons are very intelligent animals. They're smarter than cats are, but not quite as smart as species of monkeys. At night, as they are hunting for food, they use at least 51 different sounds to communicate. They eat both plants and animals and they often turn over garbage cans to look for food.

Red Fox - *Vulpes vulpes.*

RED FOX

In the wild, red foxes are active at twilight, but when they are close to human populations they become nocturnal and hunt at night. They are known for their intelligence and ability to adapt to human environments. They can jump as high as 6.5 feet in the air.

SKUNK

Skunks have an excellent way to fend off attackers. They spray them with a foul odor that lasts for days. It generally doesn't cause any real damage, but it makes the victim very uncomfortable! There are lots of different kinds of skunks, but they all have either spotted, striped, or swirled patterns of black and white fur.

Striped Skunk (Mephitis mephitis).

Just watch out if you come across any of these animals during a nighttime hike. They are wild animals so steer clear, especially from the skunk!

Awesome! Now you know more about nocturnal animals. You can find more Animal books from Baby Professor by searching the website of your favorite book retailer.

Visit
BABY PROFESSOR
EDUCATION KIDS
www.BabyProfessorBooks.com
to download Free Baby Professor eBooks
and view our catalog of new and exciting
Children's Books

www.ingramcontent.com/pod-product-compliance
Lightning Source LLC
Chambersburg PA
CBHW081958160726

47999CB00008B/2661